A Treasure Trove Of Verse

Edited by Angela Fairbrace

First published in Great Britain in 2007 by:
Forward Press Ltd.
Remus House
Coltsfoot Drive
Peterborough
PE2 9JX
Telephone: 01733 898108
Website: www.forwardpress.co.uk

SB ISBN 978-1 84418 461 3

Foreword

Forward Press was established in 1989 to provide a platform for poets to showcase their works. Today, Forward Press continues to provide an outlet for new and established poets and *A Treasure Trove Of Verse* is tribute to this.

Poetry should be interesting and, above all else, accessible to all. Forward Press publications are for all lovers of traditional verse and of the art of rhyme, as well as for those who enjoy contemporary verse. *A Treasure Trove Of Verse* showcases both styles ensuring a varied read, and proving traditional and modern do complement each other.

Contents

The Poems

My Toy Box

Out of the toy box, everyone comes to play;
My teddy bear, Lucinda doll, Bernie
Dog and Henry pussycat.

They rest all day in cot and pram
Or relax on carpeted floor.
I play with them, they are my friends,
I feed them lovely food.

They are so quiet during the day,
At night-time they come out to play,
As I slumber in my bed,
I hear music from the attic.
My loved ones dance and jig and play,
As I sleep soundly on.

Then in the morn, they rest again,
In cot and pram and Wendy house.
The shining sun - gives warmth and light.
I wash and dress - ready to play another day.

My toys are ready for cuddles and kisses,
My friends, my toys, my loved ones.

Janet Cavill

Blackbird

I parked my car at the car park's edge,
When . . . ooh!
A blackbird popped up through a hole in the hedge!
It looked around, all alert
With black, beady eyes that looked so pert;
It plucked off red berries with a little tweak
And they disappeared down its beak.
Then, without even bothering to say goodbye,
It flew off and was gone high up in the sky.

Kathy Rawstron

Rabbits Vs Squirrels

The scurrying squirrels hid their nuts in a tree
But the rabbits chasing after them still could see
As they stole the cache by squeezing through the door
When Sergeant Squirrel shouted, 'That's against the law.'

But the rabbits just grinned as they looked at the crowd,
'See here you fellows,' Sergeant Squirrel said out loud,
'You just can't come and steal a working chap's dinners!'
The ravenous rabbits grinned, for they were the winners.

'Carrots, carrots, carrots,' they chortled
As they chomped through more,
They kept on eating 'til they'd eaten a hundred and four.
Sergeant Squirrel hatched a wily plot to teach them a lesson,
'Those greedy rabbits will soon find out with whom they are messin'!'

Said the Sergeant loudly as he addressed his squad,
'We'll shake lots of pepper on the peas in the pod.'
The trick with the pepper pot didn't seem much to matter,
As battalions of rabbits recruited the old Mat Hatter.

Sergeant Squirrel wouldn't give up and wouldn't be beaten,
After all the carrots and nuts those rabbits had eaten.
He devised a special trap to catch the old Mad Hatter,
But he kept on eating and getting fatter and fatter.

At last the Sergeant found an enormous-sized copper pot
And shoving the Mad Hatter inside it he said, 'That's your lot.'
The Sergeant held up his spyglass, then he puffed and he blew,
Till the nuts fell from the tree and into the rabbit stew.

As the squadrons of squirrels ate their scrumptious dinner,
They applauded their Sergeant for being the winner.
The Sergeant just blushed all over and preened and glowed,
'Ah, shucks boys!' he said, 'Eat up, I've got another load.

But if I hadn't covered the cooking pot with that hay,
Mad Hatter and his battalion would have got clean away.'
Now the moral of this tall story is don't steal or fight,
And the squirrels and rabbits will come out of it alright.

Elizabeth A Farrelly

Lizzy Dripping

Everywhere that Lizzy goes people call out, 'Blow your nose!'
Poor Lizzy, won't it ever stop? There it goes, drip-drop, drip-drop!
Lizzy wants to go and play, but all the children run away.
Off they go, running and skipping, 'Lizzy, blow your nose,
it's dripping!'
Lizzy can't have any fun because she knows her nose will run
Drip-drop! There it goes once more, trickling and dripping on
the floor,
'Here comes Lazy Daisy, I'll ask her if she knows
Just what it is I have to do to stop my runny nose.'
But Lazy Daisy feels too tired, 'I think I'll take a nap
Come on, Lizzy, blow your nose, it's running like a tap!'
'What can I do?' cries Lizzy, drip-drop, drip-drop
Streaming from her bright red nose, plip-plop, plip-plop!
Clever Harry saunters by, let's ask him if he knows
But all that Harry has to say is, 'Lizzy, blow your nose!'
There goes Skinny Minnie looking pale and thin
She calls out, 'Lizzy, blow your nose, it's running down your chin!'
Lizzy has a bright idea, 'I know someone who'll know
I'll ask my grandad who is wise, how I can stop the flow.'
Drop-drip, drop-drip! Streaming from her nose
Running, dripping down her face like a garden hose.
Grandad listens to her tale and understands her plight
And what do you think he gives to her? A hankie, snowy-white.
'Now listen, Lizzy,' Grandad says, 'shake the hankie out
And when you feel the dripping start, use this to wipe your snout.'
Let's hope that Lizzy learns the trick which every good child knows
Always use a handkerchief to blow your runny nose!

D P Castellani

Dear Santa

That rumour of Christmas
Spreads quickly around
A hint of snow coming
To cover the ground

Christmas trees awaiting
To find a new, bright home
To glitter, give happiness
Being proud to stand alone

Bright Christmas paper
Glittering gift tags
Shops offering presents
For full shopping bags

Mince pies, chocolate logs
Creamy trifles, special treats
Gallons of fizzy drinks
All promote those rude repeats!

Well now, children, be good
Do just as you are told
We all love old Santa
Even though we are old!

Maureen Westwood O'Hara

A Nonsense Poem

On my travels far and wide across a barren land
I met a creature, oh so strange, created by God's hand.
I thought him, oh so very odd, but beautiful as well,
Perhaps you'll read my nonsense rhyme to see if you can tell
Of whom I think, of whom I see, as he spins his magic spell.

He has four chunky, large, large legs, he's not a chair or table,
He has a fifth appendage, imagine, if you are able.
A slender tail, small and neat, he's not a dog or cat,
He's large with very big front teeth, can you imagine that?
He has two enormous hearing aids, I think you call them ears.

His eyes are small and from them flow a liquid, we call tears,
His voice is strange, a trumpet sound, it booms across the plain,
He walks with family on tracks, he's really not a train.
Have you thought who he can be? I'm not at liberty to tell,
All I know is my love for him, I'll always wish him well.

Patricia Marland

Christmas Eve

So, so tired and needing to sleep
With excitement fighting the urge to peep,
I'm sure I heard a bell before
And I know there is no one at the door.
Eyes tight shut and ears tuned in,
Quilt cover pulled way up to my chin.
Lying silent and still, as still as can be,
Santa soon will visit with me!
At least I am hoping that he will be here,
Suddenly excitement has turned into fear.
What if I haven't been good today?
What if the reindeer have lost their way?
What if our chimney's not big enough?
Or worse, it's filled with soot and fluff?
Oh dear, oh dear, I heard a noise,
I'm sure I heard a clank of toys.
I must still fight that urge to peep,
I think it's time to go to sleep!

Jacqueline Madden

Wriggley, Wiggley Spider

I have a little friend
I really have to hide her
She's not very big
Just a wriggley, wiggley spider.
She likes to go a-hunting
For some little fleas
But she's got a little problem
She's got wobbly knees.

It's my wriggley, wiggley spider
And everybody knows
Just how much I love her
And every day she grows.
Someday she'll be a giant
And we'll go off to school
Everybody laughs at me
And says I'm just a fool.

She's a wriggley, wiggley spider
And I love her so
I take her to the pictures
And everywhere I go.
We go on the buses
She just enjoys the thrill
But a trip on my new skateboard
Really makes her ill.

James Peace

Squirrels

Happy squirrels, red and grey
Run and jump and climb all day
Should we get a climbing frame
And, with practise, do the same?

H H Atkinson

Brave Soldier

I march round the walls of the castle
Then cross the bridge over the moat.
I hear shouts from enemy soldiers
As they struggle to stay afloat.

I reach the huge wooden gateway
The guard's shouting, 'Halt! Who goes there?'
He lets me pass into the courtyard
Where my troops show how much they care.

'It's Sir John!' they shout and surround me,
'Our brave knight! Our leader of men!'
I'm overjoyed by their welcome,
They applaud and cheer - but then

I hear the voice of a woman
She's smiling and waving to me
As she calls from the kitchen doorway:
'Come in, Johnny, it's time for tea.'

I bid farewell to my soldiers
And I'm back in my garden, at home.
No longer a hero in armour -
Just a little boy, playing alone.

Sue Smith

All The King's Horses

All the king's horses and all the king's men,
Went down to the dogs for a flutter,
They won sixteen pounds on a dog called Eileen
And spent their winnings on Marmite and butter!

All the king's horses and all the king's men,
Were terribly posh you see!
They ate roasted prunes on gold-plated spoons
And watched dramas on the BBC.

All the king's horses and all the king's men,
Went partying off to Ibiza,
But the horses got drunk on a whisky-based punch,
Supplied by a dodgy old geezer!

All the king's horses and all the king's men,
Were extradited back to the UK,
They joined the catering navy, cooked potatoes in gravy
And sold their story for four pounds on Ebay!

Colin Wallace

Grandpapa, In Memory Ever Dear

In fond memory I dream once more of Grandpa, old and wise,
As he held my hand and walked with me, with loving in his eyes.
I was but a little one, my eyes wide with childish wonder
At the great ships lying at the quays, the dark mountains up yonder.
These were my very 'bestest' days, I loved my grandpa true
And Grandpa, though I live a hundred years, my love will be for you.

I loved our walks around the seafront; so many years have flown,
Now you have gone to another place and I have children of my own.
In memory I now look back; down the corridor of years
And in nostalgia - I knew happiness, with laughter, never tears.
I loved you, Grandpa, in your care I saw a world exciting;
Now as I travel life's pathway, your memory, it is lighting.

Patrick Glasson

If I Were A Cat

If I were a cat
I would sleep all day
I would purr and purr
And never would stray

I would help catch mice
And drink loads of milk
I would lick my fur
So it felt like silk

I would be kind and true
And miaow and miaow
I would open doors
And never would scowl

If I were a cat
I would sleep all day
I would purr and purr
And would never stray.

Anne-Marie Sane

Do Ya Wanna?

Do ya wanna see a caterpillar
Doing an Irish jig?
Do ya wanna see a pussycat
Wearing a lady's wig?
Do ya wanna see some fairies
Dancing hand in hand?
Do ya wanna see a jellyfish
Surf along the sand?
Do ya wanna see the angels
That nightly guard your bed?
Well, if you do just lie down
And rest your sleepy head.
Now close your eyes real softly
And all of this you'll see,
For you will travel to a land
The land of fantasy.

Laura Clarke

The Dragon

Dean was very tired tonight
He was so glad for his bed
He lay there for a moment
And fixed the pillow 'neath his head

A tapping at his window
Made him look that way
So he got out to have a look
And to his great dismay

There was a dragon breathing fire
And clawing at the pane
His feet had toenails two feet long
There were bad things on his brain

His tail had barbs upon it
He could strike a nasty blow
If he got the chance to use it
But Dean was brave you know

He opened up the window
And to the dragon's great surprise
Dean punched him with a deadly blow
And fly-sprayed both his eyes

The dragon didn't have a chance
He fell down at a rate
His fire went out, his toenails shrunk
And he was eaten by a snake.

Joyce Newton

Alien From Outer Space

I am an alien
I come from outer space
I get a horrible fright
When I see your human face

I came down to Earth
To see my best friend
I didn't know you were so ugly
It sent me around the bend

I've only got one leg
You have got two
I haven't got any ears
So I can't hear you

I carry a ray gun
It shines a bright light
If you look into it
It'll damage your sight

I'm covered in dirt
It's a total disgrace
It doesn't suit you humans
So I'm going back to space!

Rachael Turnage

Playground Blues

I'm in the playground alone again
Trying to look busy with my phone,
Cos Katy who was my new best friend
Has left me all alone.

Any Mummy says I'm not to mind,
That Katy's just a butterfly
And that she really isn't very kind
And I mustn't cry.

And Luce's dad is ever so famous,
Or he was, once, and she's got a pony.
She's staying tonight at Katy's house
And I'm feeling so lonely.

And next week, it's the Christmas show -
Katy and I were going to sing,
But a duet for one is so silly you know
And they're all whispering.

Simone Mansell Broome

Places In My Book

When I grow up to be a man
I will travel foreign lands
To visit places to have a look
At all the places in my book.
I will see the mountains of Nepal
Then visit the vineyards of Portugal
I will see the leaning tower in Italy
Maybe the jungle men of New Guinea.
Into deepest Congo I will go
Then to Greenland to see an Eskimo
I will see a Geisha in Japan
After that, eat a bowl of rice with a Chinaman.
In Australia I will see a kangaroo
Then while in Mali, visit Timbuktu
In Egypt I will see the pyramids in the sand
Then go see the Zulus in Swaziland.
I will see the llamas of Peru
This is what I am going to do
When I visit places to have a look
At all the places in my book.

Cavan Campbell

The Tooth Fairy

The fairies were sitting talking
Of jobs they had to do
One of them stood to tell the others
About a little girl she knew
'This little girl is called Mollie
And her first tooth has come out
So tonight I have to make a call
To Mollie's house
There is no doubt.'
So in the middle of the night
When all were fast asleep
The fairy went to Mollie's house
And in her window she did peep
Taking her magic wand
She waved it in the air
Turning Mollie's tooth
Into money lying there
Knowing Mollie would be pleased
She fluttered her wings and was gone
Telling herself that of course
She would be back again before long.

Daphne Fryer

Night Horrors

A squeak from the wainscot
A creak from the stair
Scratching in the attic space and
A crawling feeling in my hair.

I saw a creeping shadow there
As I lay in bed and quake
I hid under my bedspread
All of a shiver and a shake.

There's a tapping at the window
So I close my eyes up tight
What's that moaning at the casement?
It must be some awful sight.

The bedroom door seems far away
The room has changed I know
My heart is pounding in my ears
I'm fearful of this unseen foe.

The curtains billow gently out
Letting through a silvery shoon
It floods my room with spectral light
Can it really only be the moon?

If I don't move, if I don't scream
Perhaps the 'thing' will fade away
I'll hold my breath and count to ten
And wish for night to turn to day.

Jean Selmes

The Witch

There was an old witch who sat down and cried,
For her broomstick had upped upon her to ride
Over the sailing moon in the sky
And left her behind to weep and to cry,
With only her cat to comfort her then
She knew she would not ride the sky again.

So she went to the fair in the market town,
Where she bought a sieve to sail on the sea,
And knew she was right, as right as could be
As she started at once to sail far away,
To the sad lost rim of the dying day.

Now she rides on the tempest
Waves spume tossed, over the giant oceans lost,
Through calm and blizzard, rain and hail,
Screeching and screaming in frenzied gale.
She touches the ships alone who dare
To sail to the edge of her wild despair.

Then on she twists with malice bright,
To darken the world and quench the light.
In blinding sleet and stinging hail
She turns and turns in the teeth of a gale,
Gloating at all that she has done,
While mocking the dying beams of the sun.

The croaking sea birds flee her face,
And sea-bound monsters beg for grace
As she rides out time with no earthly bond,
To the wide world's end and to that beyond.

D M Neu

My Scary Spider

I have this scary spider,
Who lives here in my pocket,
It has eight,
Long,
Hairy legs,
That scamper,
Scurry
And hurry,
A big, fat, juicy body,
Splattered with spots,
Of pink,
Yellow,
Green,
And blue,
That shine,
And sparkle,
In the sunshine,
And funny,
Pointy,
Fangs,
That drip
And snap,
With goo.

During the daytime,
When I'm at school,
It weaves,
Thin,
Fragile,
Strands of web,
And stands,
Proudly,
Inspecting,
Closely,
With the big eyes upon its head.

At home,
I like to keep it,
In an empty matchbox,
By the window,
It's filled with fluffy,
Comfy,
Balls,
Of soft cotton wool,
That it uses as its bed.
I have to close it,
When he sleeps,
'Cause he snores so very loud,
He snorts,
And grunts,
And drones away,
So I have to keep it shut.

When I wake up,
I say, 'Good morning Mr Spider,'
And then,
When I switch off my light,
At night,
I whisper, 'Mr Spider,
Goodnight.'

When I show my sister,
She screams,
And runs,
With fright,
Grassing out to Mummy
And gets me grounded,
For the night.

When I show my brother,
He prods,
And pokes,
And pulls,
His face,
Filled with glee.

I did try,
To stick the leg back on,
But now,
My spider makes do,
With only,
Seven.
One day,
I think I'll name my spider,
But for now,
I like to watch,
And wait,
To see what he can do,
Then,
You see,
I'll know just what to call him,
My scary spider,
And me.

Peter Morris-Webb

Nonsense

Tomorrow we went to school
And last year we will leave.
Our teacher reprimanded us
For we will tear a sleeve.

It's dark to find our way about,
The sun shines while we sleep,
We always walk upon our hands,
And climb up to the deep.

Trees stand proud upon their leaves,
Their roots wave in the air.
The rain falls upward from the Earth
And everything is dry.

We skate upon the raging sea,
And hear the fishes dancing.
Yesterday will soon arrive,
Tomorrow has just passed.

J H Jenkins

The Frog

A frog am I who used to be
A prince who dressed so splendidly
I was handsome, I was rich
But then there came a wicked witch
Who loathed to see me kind and gay
Made me as I am today
A frog, an ugly, croaking frog
Who sits all day upon a log
And waits upon a maiden kind
Who one day in my face may find
Something worthy of a kiss
And then this gentle-hearted miss
Will cure the curse that's so long lain
And I will be a prince again.

Gordon Andrews

Just Spinning

World, world, I'm tired of your spinning
In fact I'm feeling quite ill
Can't you stop for a while and let me get off?
I'll jump right back when I've had enough

'Nay, nay,' said the world, 'I cannot stop
I revolve on an axis with a bit of a wobble
So you'll stay in my care with some moments to share
Or I might wobble right off and ditch us all in the trough.'

Doris Hoole

Three Million Two Hundred Years And Two Weeks Ago

Last night I was told a story and I want you all to know
About a dinosaur and his family, it happened many long years ago
The dinosaur was grazing by a swamp, lazily chewing his cud
Looking down past some trees into the misty, bubbling mud
The dinosaur was happy and nothing did he fear
Suddenly from that swamp, some bubbles did appear
As he watched that swamp, it bubbled madly and then
First there was one and before he knew it there were ten
Those bubbles moved together, suddenly they became just one
That dinosaur shook his head and looked up at the morning sun
Thinking that his father had told him many years before
That his father had seen this, but he thought it just some folklore
I'd better check this out, so he moved a little near
Now from that swamp, more and more bubbles did appear
Again they moved together, like he had seen in the past
Lazily chewing a branch from a tree, knowing this would not last
But thousands of bubbles did appear, and now they moved to ground
As that dinosaur looked he did find, hundreds more were all around
Then as the sun began to rise, those bubbled shed their skin
How was that poor dinosaur to know, that mankind is to begin?
He looked at the far and distant sea and there he saw many,
many more
Suddenly there were more and more bubbles coming fast to the
distant shore
The dinosaur looked at his family, he gazed at them with pride
How was that dinosaur to know, many bubbles would come in
with each tide?
Now those bubbles had shapes and some even moved into a
small huddle
Those new creatures were now drinking from a large new puddle
Oh, how was that poor dinosaur to know, that man's time had begun?
That dinosaur began to laugh; he knew he would not be here for long
For those bubbles now dancing, could it be? They are singing an
Irish song
Yes, that is the story I was told as I lay sick in my bed
It is the story true of Ireland, and that is what my grandfather has
just said.

Francis McGarry

Sid The Shark

Lonely Sid the shark
Sat all day at home
He had no friends that called round
He was always on his own

So one day he decided
He would go out and make a pal
He swam around all day long
And found himself a friend called Sal

Sal was a pretty sea horse
And she was lonely too
She spent all day in her house
With nothing much to do

So Sid and Sal became best of friends
Everywhere they went
The disco, café, cinema too
Until all their money they had spent

So Sid decided to cook dinner
He told Sal to call round for eight
So Sal got all dressed up and ready
For her special date

They both sat down for dinner
And had way too much to drink
Side sat back and smiled at Sal
Then gave her a little wink

Sal fluttered her eyelids
And her cheeks went rosy-red
She lent forward to give Sid a kiss
But he gobbled her up instead

See Sid had a slight confession
He thought he should reveal
He didn't really care much for Sal's company
And sea horse was his favourite meal!

Amy Louise Clayton

Peter, The Park Keeper's Pen

My name is Peter, I am the park keeper's pen,
I am placed behind his ear and flicked on now and again.
There's lots of writing to do
When we tally up the stock,
We need overalls, garden equipment,
Brushes and the occasional lock.
The lock is for the shed
Where Parky keeps his stuff,
We use it mostly every day
In the rain, the sunshine and even if the weather's rough.
I am always wedged behind Parky's ear,
I am as important to him, as well as his gear.
Yes, Parky and me are very good friends,
My name is Peter . . . the park keeper's special pen.

Mary Plumb

The Five-Legged Cat

There was a cat that had five legs
And ears that lit up pink
His eyes were huge and brightest blue
Too huge to even blink

His whiskers were like handlebars
They just stuck out for miles
They helped him keep his balance
When he was on the tiles

His tail was like a bottle brush
That just stuck out behind
He was the most unusual cat
That you could ever find

When he wanted feeding
He didn't say miaow
Instead he started mooing
As if he were a cow

He had a tiny, round, black nose
For sniffing out the mice
And though he looked so very strange
He really was quite nice.

Barbara Hampson

Accident

Mummy, don't be cross with me, I didn't *mean* to do it,
I only meant to look at it, but by mistake, I threw it!

You say to leave your things alone, but my fingers seem to touch
Without me realising that they're up to very much.

I can tell you're sad to see how many pieces this is in
(Although Daddy always said it would look better in the bin)

So I'll save my pocket money without tantrums, sulks or tears
And you shall have another one, in six or seven years.

Oh Mummy, I'm so glad that you are giving me this cuddle,
I'm sorry that my hands and feet and brain get in a muddle.

Toni Dinsdale

A Little Girl's Dream

As I lay in my bed last night
Gazing up at all the stars
I wondered what life would be like
If I lived on Jupiter or Mars.
Would alarm clocks wake me up
And would I have to go to school?
Would the children have school reports?
Would they be told to listen to teacher's rule?
What would the weather be like?
Perhaps very hot, or maybe too cold
And if I was ever a little naughty
Would Mum and Dad still scold?
I bet there are no rules up there
Just playing and eating ice cream each day
Nobody to tell me to eat all my greens
When I push my plate away.
Excuses for regularly getting dirty
I'm sure I could find lots more
Reasons for never tidying my room
Funny how things end up on the floor.
Dad says I am just mischievous
And I'll grow out of it in time
But I'm not too sure if Mum agrees
She says, up the wall she's going to climb.

Judith Watts

Going To School

I sit in my window and watch the children
Going on their way to school,
Some are walking very quickly
While others are playing the fool.

A group of boys are coming along
Talking together in a huddle,
They did not hear me call out to them
Too late, they've all walked into a big puddle.

Here come two little girls holding hands,
Oh dear, I hope they are not going to be late,
As they have stopped to look at a garden
Through some big iron gates.

I can hear the school bell ringing
Some of them quicken their pace,
Others are still dawdling
With no intention of making haste.

Then suddenly they all take flight
Their satchels banging their backs as they ran,
I do hope they get to school in time
Before the gates are shut with a clang.

Now all is peace and quiet again
God bless their little souls,
I pray that when they are old enough
They manage to reach their goals.

Phyllis Ing

A Raggedy House

A raggedy house, a secret mouse
A worm without any shoes
A rickety book, a linseed hook
A hamster playing its tunes
This is the place where tails are chased
And nothing is coloured in blue

A knitted lead, a dirty sleeve
A cockroach eating a cake
A glitter parade, a fountain cave
A circle rolling in goo
This is the room without any gloom
And magic is made with a shoe

A knock on the ceiling, a hidden meaning
A jigsaw dancing with leaves
A broken down bed, an indoor shed
A cloud with a tickly sneeze
This is the street where polar bears meet
And wizards say too-da-loo

A wobbly stick, an up and a hic
A chewing gum stuck to a tree
A marigold car, a chef's guitar
A picture frame counting to three
This is the town where nothing falls down
And even the soil is free

So if you hear click, stood next to a brick
And the wires all turn to stare
If the plates all jangle, and Eskimos dangle
Then maybe you might be there
For this is the place where time is a waste
And nothing is gobbledy goo.

Lucy Thomas

Christmas Party

When we leave the party
Will there be a moon?
Will we hear the piper
Play our favourite tune?

A world of white surrounds us
And in the floating flakes
We can hear the piper
And sounds he makes.

I can see his tall black hat
His suit of crimson bright,
Trousers tucked inside his boots
Dancing quick and light.

Will he meet our snowman
To ask him for a dance?
Shall our man in white
Pass a smiling glance?

The piper and the snowman
Are dancing in the snow
When they stop to catch their breath
Then where will they go?

Across the field
Around the hill
Until they stop
The trees are still.
The sheep have gone
Into the barn
They are safe and warm
Like Jesus was when he was born
Snowflakes touch my face
I cannot see the piper
Can he see me?

Do you think he is hungry?
Does he like mince pies?
And squidgy cakes
And chocolate biscuits
Like Mummy makes?

When I go to bed
I'll lie and think of him
Will he have some presents?
Does he have a stocking full to the brim?
Will he knock on our front door?
Can he stay for tea?

I can see my stocking
On the bottom of my bed
Daddy is in the rocking chair
In Mummy's place instead
I am waiting for my story
And snuggle up with Ted.

Would the piper listen?
Where has he gone?
I do not know
Is he cold and hungry out there
In the freezing snow?

Ann Wardlaw

Back To School

Our holidays are finished and now it's back to school
We're going to learn new things, we're going to learn new rules.
We'll talk about history and geography and laws
About heroes and villains fighting for a cause.
But now I must be quiet and listen carefully
Because I can see my teacher looking angrily back at me.

D E Rothwell

King Rat

I'm not *really fat*
Just a rather portly old rat
Who will guard his precious domain
Against any predatory cat.

When I see a feline
Coming down the side
My eyes have a steel-edge glint
And are football pitch wide.

If they think for a minute
They can get one over on me
I'll show them who's the ruler round here
I'll soon make them flee!

There's a strange one
Who occasiónally trespasses here
And doesn't seem to possess
The usual tomcat fear.

He advances towards me
With a gingerly tread
And a pitter-patter sound
Just down there, by the shed.

I only caught the blur
Of a baseball bat.
The lights went out
And I went . . . *splat!*

David Paul Heath

Sophie's Song

I've got a dolls' house. It's rather silly.
There's one wall missing so it must get chilly.
The dolls keep warm staying in bed.
There's lots of room. Like I said.
Santa must have brought all the furniture he'd got,
two double beds, three single beds, a cradle, a cot,
a lounge suite, a dining suite like in a proper house,
a high chair, a grand piano and a plastic mouse.
If only Santa'd realised, there are only two rooms here,
he might have given me that kit to make home-made beer.

Rosemary Benzing

I Spy The Fly

Under the slide I shivered
Whatever will my fate be?
I only walked over the surface
Kicking legs, having fun, feeling free.

However did all this happen?
I thought I was in control,
It is worse than being swatted
Or in a jar with a lid and a hole.

Wish I'd never seen the window
Or even the wide open door,
And who the heck left nibbles
Right here on the dining room floor?

Of course I'm going to take some
What's a hungry guy supposed to do?
I just didn't expect so much anger
From someone as timid as you.

Your eye and mine making contact
As you peer through your microscope,
Looking for germs that cause diseases
Unlucky! We flies don't have any, *I hope.*

We know they do, don't we?

Dorren Dulally

Toys

I have a big new bicycle,
Painted red with saddle bag too.
My bike has a bell and four wheels,
It could be a tank, or a battleship blue.
New toys aren't made for invention,
Give me old things for games of pretence -
The shed down the garden is a hangar,
A spade is a bomber, a fork a fighter,
Wheelbarrow an aircraft carrier.
A rake is a Hawker, a hoe a Harrier.
I fly my planes around our garden,
I am the pilot of them all, I am the best.
I usually play this when my sister has a rest.

Jane McCarty

Re: Cycling

Like a windmill, like a corkscrew,
Like a circle on the ground,
Like a whisk or like a dancer
My wheels are pirouetting round.

It's a journey through a legend,
It's a time upon the wing,
It's a Samurai in Iceland,
It's a song beyond the wind.

I've a whistling at my eardrums,
Flashing faces, mountains, streams;
Children pointing fingers,
Laugh like gardens born of dreams.

And I'm hurtling through a forest,
Where the boughs are made of gold,
And I'm dashing over oceans,
Over waves and seas untold.

Onwards fighting Martians,
Through a lake of molten fire,
Spraying mud and guts and glory,
On my T-shirt with my tyres.

Past the baker and the schoolyard,
Past the long abandoned train,
Past the farm and Dog and Pony,
Past the world, then back again.

Felicity Perera

How To Ride A Sea Horse

Go to a lonely tropical beach, where
the mild air welcomes you, wraps
you in its warm embrace. Wade
into the silky green water and
prepare for a gradual sea change,
shrinking to a frail sliver of self.
The sea horse, a tiny chessman, waits
to take you to unfamiliar deeps.
Grasp his seaweed reins and mount,
your feet on his body's bony ridges
like stirrups. Cling on while he swims upright,
sinks through translucent waves to the sea floor.
Pectoral fins whirr like tiny motors
as you drift among wondrous sea creatures,
mysterious caverns, vanished cities.
Dream of finding the gates of lost Atlantis.

Joan Lees

Lilly's Words

This morning Lilly awoke
Yawning as she spoke
Her words spread out
Right out of her mouth
And hit her dad on the nose

This morning everyone knew
That Lilly's words were like the flu
They twisted and turned
Rolled and churned
Until each street was through

This morning everyone hid
As Lilly's words spread
She opened her mouth
And more came out
The words everyone dread

The morning had almost gone
And Lilly was still going strong
With her mouth so wide
Her words filled the sky
Nothing could stop them reaching up high

Something had to be done
Thought the lady at number one
And so with her pillow
So fluffy and soft
No one could stop themselves nodding off

So that's the end of the story
She had fallen asleep still talking
The town was now quiet
And everywhere silent
Until someone had noticed her snoring.

Emma Macdougall

Kirsty's Kite

Kirsty's kite was purple and blue
shaped like a dragon, you could see right through;
it wiggled and waggled as it soared in the air,
sometimes being naughty, it dived down just to scare.
children and grown-ups would run out of the way,
some shrieking, some laughing, but all loving the day
when Kirsty's kite, which was purple and blue,
soared into the air wagging its

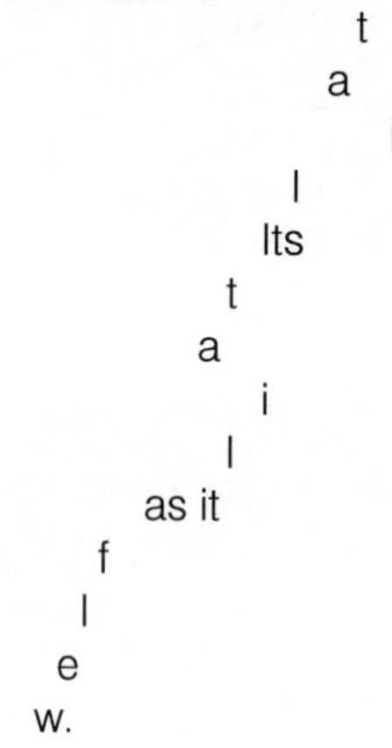

t
a
i
l
Its
t
a
i
l
as it
f
l
e
w.

B J Walklate

Questions

Mother, where do the stars go
when day comes over the hill?

My dear, though you cannot see them
the stars are shining still.
Their light cannot compete
with the powerful light of day
but they never stop their shining . . .
they never go away.

Mother, where does the wind go
when it's calm upon our hill?

My dear, though you cannot feel it
the wind is blowing still.
It has left us for a mountain
or a leafy river bend
but it never stops its blowing . . .
it never has an end.

Mother, where does the rain go
when the air is hot and dry?

My dear, though you cannot touch it
it's somewhere in the sky.
Go looking for a rainbow
over hill and plain
and where you find its colours
you'll also find the rain.

Carol Don Ercolano (New Zealand)

Spooky Sounds

One Hallowe'en night, Spooky Sounds was busy,
When he bumped his head and then felt dizzy.

Where to put his sounds? He couldn't remember,
All to be placed before the 1st of November.

Tonight was the night to make kids jump,
With spooky whisperings and the occasional bump.

In a spirited rush, he dashed here and there,
Putting spooky sounds almost anywhere.

He put:
A crash in your mash
A laugh in your bath
The ouch on your couch
The roar behind your door
A boo in your shoe
A thud in your hood
A guffaw in your drawer
A howl in your towel
Hoots in your boots
Knocks in your socks
A sigh in your pie
A hiss in your dish
Bumps in your pumps
Nags in your bags
Some whams in your jams
A scrape on your cake
Hums in your buns
A scrunch in your lunch
A weeheee in your tea
Some screams in your beans
A boom on your spoon
A cough in your loft
A mutter in your butter
And squeaks in your sheets

Now, when things go bump in the mid of night,
Don't be alarmed, don't take flight.
Snuggle under your covers and listen good,
Is that Spooky Sounds in *your* neighbourhood?

George, Anna and Mum

The Sandcastle

My mummy, daddy, Teddy and me,
Went on holiday by the sea.
With my bucket and my spade,
A great big sandcastle we made.

Around this we dug a moat,
Deep enough to sail a boat.
A drawbridge was our way in
To defend our castle we would begin.

The waves like an enemy would creep,
Into the walls of the moat so steep.
Onto the castle turret they sped,
Retreat we must, me and Ted.

Another castle we did make,
Still the sea did overtake.
All those waves danced with glee,
At their victory over Teddy and me.

Emily Rose

1 Red Apple

1 red apple falling from a tree,
2 brown squirrels yelling, *'Yippee!'*
3 black ants nibbling on the core,
when they're done, there's nothing more.
4 blue birds flying in the sky,
the scent of the apple makes them stop by.
5 white butterflies join them on the ground,
6 orange cats chase them around and around.
7 yellow ducks saying, *quack, quack, quack,*
follow their mother in a row to the snack.
8 green grasshoppers, hop, hop, hop,
to see what it was that fell from the top.
9 grey spiders slowly, slowly crawl,
to find that there's nothing left at all.
10 more apples fall from the tree,
now everyone is as happy as can be.

Crystal L Grose

The Magpie

A magpie came into the house
And ate my lunch for me
Although he's not invited
I expect him back for tea

He stole my red pyjamas
And he thieved my baseball cap
And he stole my father's toupee
While my father took a nap

He stole a clock, a teaspoon
And a picture from the wall
He used the phone to ring his friend
And not a local call

He went into my bedroom
And he surfed the Internet
I've really tried to catch him
But I haven't caught him yet

He frightened the Alsatian dog
And made my mother cry
The goldfish needs some counselling
But can't remember why

He went into the living room
And sat down in a chair
I know this, as I went in
And there's feathers everywhere

He even did his washing
And we really can't have that
So we went down to the pet shop
And we came back with a cat.

Nigel Cowdery

The Aliens Are Coming!

The aliens are coming!
I can see their lights outside;
Shining through my curtains,
I think that I must hide!

Perhaps if I keep very still
And hide under my bed,
The aliens won't find me there
And go elsewhere instead.

But what is that? A shadow,
Being cast upon the wall?
Black and scary, with horns on top
And now it's growing tall!

Suppose I took a little peep
And something scary stared;
Straight back at me, into my eyes,
Would I be very scared?

No! I am a hero!
I like to stand my ground.
I'll fight the aliens and monsters
Until there are none around!

There is just one thing left now,
That is worrying in my head;
It's the vision of my mum's cross face,
If I'm not asleep in bed!

Tracey Lynn Birchall

Teddy And I

In the garden where we play
Teddy and I had fun today
Together we put toys away
It's the evening of our day

Time to climb up the stairs
Then teddy and I say our prayers
To our Father up above
For His never-ending love
Let no dream give us a fright
Bless our waking with sunlight

God bless Mum and Dad
Gran, Grandad, our pets too
Teddy and I both ask You
Keep them safe all night through
Teeth we brushed, prayers we said
Now on a pillow lay our head
Safely tucked up in our bed
We are warm and have been fed
Although outside blows a storm
Teddy is in here with me
Warm and safe we shall be!
For a day of fun and sky of blue
And loving us whatever we do
Teddy and I both thank You.

Sheila Walters

Mother

Spring: Sails in on fragile shells
lavender-blue of bluebells
her tears are falling rain
tissue leaves bursting again

Summer: Rides sea-sprayed mare
seapinks in her hair
her cloak is flowery wind
unshod, and golden skinned

Autumn: Arrives, tossing down acorn
gilds cobs in fields of corn
brown arms in tattered sleeves
sweeping away rainbowed leaves

Winter: Walking in silvery shoes
silence left behind as she moves
stills river into an icy flow
leaves no footprints in snow.

T Webster

The Giant

The giant in the tower
Laid down his weary head
He could not lay his body down
So he rested it instead

Deliver me from anguish
This size of me portrays
Let me be small again
So that I can sing and play

As a child nobody loved him
So he thought he would conquer all
Overcoming his enemies
He fought until he was tall.

Beverley Forster

Anaconda

I'm kinda fonda my anaconda
I keep him in the bath,
I got him from the pet shop
Last Tuesday for a laugh.

He's greeny-brown and rather fat,
His length I couldn't guess,
He stretches up the banisters
Like something from Loch Ness.

He's got a friendly personality
And likes to grip your hand,
He's smooth and warm
And gives me hugs,
Which I really think is grand.

I've told him not to flick his tongue,
That it's considered rude,
He simply takes no notice
And swallows down his food.

He's kinda fonda rats to eat
But doesn't sniff at mice,
I serve them on a bed of slugs
Which he prefers to rice.

He doesn't grumble
Or hog the telly,
He doesn't smell or snore,
And when you run out of orange juice,
He squeezes you some more!

In fact, I think he's my best friend
As anacondas go,
Perhaps you should get one too
They've got one left you know.

Susan E Thomas

Our Class

Red-faced Robin Rose,
Never ever caught a cold,
But always picked his nose.

Dreary Diane Dare,
Round her little finger rolled
Her long, straight, mousy hair.

Silent Stuart Shreeve,
Pulled his sweater in a fold,
Then sat and sucked the sleeve.

Portly Philip Phipp,
Slipped off his chair and then told
The class he'd bit his lip.

Dozy Derek Denne,
With tasks his brain could not hold,
Stared and twiddled his pen.

Ace scorer Trevor Trace,
Dummies on the pitch he sold.
In class he looked at space!

Crafty Colin Clipp,
Cut some paper, then behold,
Jill's hair was given a snip!

Naughty Nathan Nowt,
Teacher often had to scold,
Since he kept shouting out!

Brainy Bill Beecher,
Through hard tests the know-all strolled . . .
Son of Class 6 teacher!

Children in our class,
Are nuggets of tarnished gold!
Their behaviour? I pass!

Bob Crittenden

Under The Covers

Buttons missing where the eyes used to be
Straw peeking out for everyone to see
Arms and legs and ears replaced
By jacket, jumpers, all made from waste

My torch has colours green and red
I switch it on when I am in bed
I slip under the covers so no one can see
It's a secret between my teddy and me

Teddy Snowy and Panda Bear
Upstairs, downstairs, everywhere
When it's time to go to bed
I take my favourite bear called Ted

I love my little teddy bear
All my secrets with him I share
He is my friend, don't you know?
I take him with me wherever I go.

Gerard Jones

Transformation

A caterpillar sat on a redcurrant bush
And a very fine fellow was he:
With stripes of yellow, white, orange and black,
An eye-catching fellow to see!

Now somebody spied him there on the bush
And brought him inside in a jar
(With plenty of leaves), and said to two boys,
'I've brought you a friend, here you are!'

The boys kept an eye on their jazzy new friend
And gave him some fresh leaves to eat . . .
Then one day he just wasn't there anymore -
But a strange ball, no stripes and no feet!

Time went by, till one day the boys' mum
Said, 'Come, take a look - here you are!'
And with wings of yellow, white, orange and black -
There's a beautiful moth in the jar!

The moral of this little stripy tale
Is as clear as a shining star:
When you're thinking that something of beauty is lost,
Remember that moth in the jar!

Mary Dimond

Furry Creatures

I love to watch the squirrels
As they dash up in the trees.
I watch them speeding down again;
They never scrape their knees!

All squirrels are inquisitive,
Always looking out for food.
They steal the wild birds' peanuts;
Now, don't you think that's rude?

But they are so cute and furry,
With those lovely bushy tails.
They are nicer than most insects
And those slimy garden snails!

Ann Potkins

The Busy Bee

I am a busy bee
It is so lovely for me,
To sit upon the flowers
And collect the pollen,
For the queen bee who
Waits for me.

She makes up the honey
Boys and girls like for tea,
So tasty with warm crumpets
I like being a busy bee,
So when out playing
Look out for me,
The busy bee, that's me!

Rose Ellis

Brian The Bicycle

Brian the bicycle has shiny round wheels,
He costs little to keep, as he doesn't eat meals!
His bones are of metal and painted in style
He'll be your best friend, for mile after mile.

When you feel like a journey, just sit on his seat,
Find his two pedals, just right for your feet!
Put one hand on each of his handlebar grips
Now you are ready for one of your trips.

With a turn of the pedals, you get underway,
Where will you get to, this bright sunny day?
Perhaps by the river, or pond . . . feed the ducks?
Or a quiet country lane, far away from big trucks.

Wherever you journey, the choice is your own
And when you are ready, you can then turn back home.
Be kind to your Brian . . . your bicycle friend
And who knows, in time . . . where your journey may end?

F J Paton

Pay Attention

Why is the teacher raising her voice?
We'd better behave now. We have no choice.

Sat down cross-legged. Hands on our knees
Not daring to move. I hope I don't sneeze.

'It wasn't me, Miss, who started the fight,
It was him, he hit me, with all his might.'

'But it was an accident, when I hit him,
I was just showing my friend how to swim.'

'What!' screamed the teacher. 'Swimming in science?
That's very stupid, you could hit an appliance.'

'What if the Bunsen burner had fell?
The whole place afire, then no tale you could tell.'

'I want two hundred lines, saying 'don't mess about,
Cause danger to others and make teacher shout'.

'As for you hitting back, you're in detention
and the rest of the class, better now pay attention.'

Julie Steadman

The Great Spider Steeplechase

You will never guess what I saw last week
While I was out playing hide-and-seek
I peeped round the corner, I had to look twice
There saddled on spiders sat six little mice

The mice looked so nice in their little suits
On their tiny feet they wore spurred boots
A crowd gathered round, they were going to race
Have you heard of the great spider steeplechase?

A frog shouted out, 'Let the races begin'
As he spoke these words he banged on a tin
The spiders and riders took to their marks
They started so fast, I thought I saw sparks

First over the jump was the mouse wearing red
He was riding the spider called Fuzzy Old Fred
Coming up behind Fred, Borris ran for the lead
But he took the corner at disastrous speed

His third leg on the right got tangled with Fred's
The spiders crashed down in a huge pile of legs
The next spider along, well he just could not stop
As the pile got closer he landed on top

As more turned the corner the pile got bigger
It ended at last with a spider called Trigger
Trigger went slowly, he was the oldest of all
But he used his brains so he would not fall

He had plenty of time to run round the heap
So he did not get tangled in legs, boots and feet
Trigger was the winner, the best of the lot
And as for the others, they are still there in knots.

Helen Matts

My Special Toy

I feel a special tenderness towards my Mickey Mouse,
I have him here, I have him there, he's all around my house.
I look into his happy face and know that through the years,
I shall carry him from place to place, his hands to wipe my tears.
But I'm not always sad as I look upon his smile,
When I am down, he makes me think life really is worthwhile.
I'm glad my mum bought Mickey, as he goes where're I go,
When I'm travelling in the car or on a plane,
In my pocket when I'm in the snow.
He's never far away from me; he'll always be my friend,
I'll care for him and mend him until the very end.

Anita Mackenzie

The Snow Fairy

One early winter morning I woke up to see it snowing
My garden covered glistening white, so bright that it was glowing

I rubbed my eyes in disbelief at the snowy winter scene
Last night before I closed my eyes, the garden it was green

I watched from through my window, the softest, silent snowfall
When I saw a single snowflake rest upon the garden wall
And on it I did see a fairy sitting there
She was wrapped in whitest fur, silver feathers in her hair

From the wall she gently flew down to the snowy-covered grass
She wore a silver dress and slippers made of glass
Her eyes were snowy-blue like you'd never ever seen
The most enchanting frost-like fairy
She must have been the snow queen.

From her tiny purse she took fairy dust into her hand
And sprinkled all around the magic silver sand

Then the air around turned cold, the sky was icy-blue
The snow queen left my garden and off she flew to you
She drifts down from her snowflake, takes a feather from her hair
And leaves a winter wish behind a trail of silver air.

Brenda McCallum

Vengeance Is Sweet

Speeding frothy waters
Running alongside
I was looking out the porthole
All pent up inside
Through the porthole reaching
Frantic and despaired
Ted was lost forever
Riding on the waves.

Brothers are a nuisance
Never wrong - just right
Why did he have to do it?
I only took one ride
On his poxy tractor
When we were called inside
A crash, a bang, then a wallop
Story is now told.

Angry brother's vengeance came about twofold!
Grim-faced and fuming
He held on to my ted
And as I protested strongly
He threw poor teddy in
But my revenge was sweeter
He knew not till this day
That a handful of his precious soldiers
Had battled with the waves!

A C Yap-Morris

My Picnic

Lots of scrumptious things to eat
And twiggy things with wiggy feet,
One got on the plate and made my sister scream!
Then my auntie on my mother's side
Told us about a film and my mum cried
So Dad and I went fishing in the stream.

We caught some weird things in our nets
And Dad had a couple of cigarettes -
He gave up last year and so I mustn't tell!
My little brother scratched his leg
And we found this little tiny egg
All brown and speckled, and a snail's shell.

We got five acorns and when they grow
We'll have massive oak trees in a row -
We'll plant them far apart, not close together!
We can go next week if it doesn't rain,
Saw a smashing sunset from the train,
And I think that picnics are the best thing ever!

Tina Molli

Autumn Blaze

Autumn is here, near and dear,
Rubies, lemons, oranges, rich browns,
A riot of colour comes tumbling down.
Trees are standing, wearing their crowns.

The fields a riot of scarlet fire blazes,
Gone is the season of flowers and daisies.
Rustling and bustling come falling leaves,
In the whistling wind make a melody dance in the breeze.

Slender and tall, each tree stands proudly,
Wearing her brown garments, adorned in gold.
Fluttering shawl of crimson rubies falling to the ground,
Laden with jewel-leaves, she wears autumn, her crown.

The leaves are her children, Wynken and Blynken;
Flipping and rolling, swaying and singing, dancing and jumping.
Wynken and Blynken are skipping, hopping and playing beneath
a rainbow,
The leaves are a pot full of honey, the pride of their mummies.

Joy is the feeling, these leaves are feeling,
With ease and pleasure, the trees are seeing,
The leaves are the crest and colour of joy;
Blessing the dreary world with their golden kisses.

Autumn a beacon, Autumn a fire, Autumn a flare, and a thing
to inspire;
Autumn is like a symbol of hope; Autumn is like a guiding light;
Autumn is like a signal to us, that God really is, all around us.

Naomi Craster-Chambers

A Dog's Life

Rufus was a lazy dog who got so very fat
He didn't have the energy to chase the local cat
All he did the whole day long was lie beside the fire
And even chewing biscuits was enough to make him tired

His master told him, 'Rufus, you're really out of shape
You'll have to cut down on the food and try to lose some weight
You're going to have to face it, you need a doggy diet
I've seen one in the pet shop and I'm off right now to buy it'

So Rufus chewed on wholemeal bones and healthy food like that
He even did some exercise to try and lose the fat
And after several months went by he got so fit and lean
That no one would have ever guessed how fat he once had been

Now Rufus is so healthy he can run for hours and hours
He chases after motorbikes and chases after cars
He's faster than a greyhound, of that there is no doubt
And now the local cat stays home when Rufus is about.

Ken Grimason

Born Again, (And Again And Again?)

A caterpillar crawled, with some dispatch,
Out from the egg from which it hatched.
One day it felt distinctly odd,
So curled up on the leaf it trod.
Its chrysalis to a butterfly said,
'How do you know when you are dead?'
The butterfly thought and then replied,
'I've no idea. I've never died.
But, pray ask someone else, I beg.'
Then fluttered off to lay an egg.

John Beazley

Fat Cat

Fat cat
Lazy cat
Fast asleep
On the mat

Eyes a-blinking
Legs a-twitching
Can't you reach
The bit that's itching?

Bet you are dreaming
About that mouse
The one you chased
All round the house

Upstairs, downstairs
Through Mum's kitchen
I heard her scream
Real ear-splitting

She chased you out
With a stick
I've never seen
You move so quick

Fat cat
Lazy cat
Stay asleep
On the mat

It's much safer
When you dream
Than when you make
Our mother scream.

Christine Collins

Jimmy And The Frog Pond

Young Jimmy McGlish can swim like a fish;
He glides through the water, swish, swish, swish, swish.

'Don't swim in the pond with the frogs,' his mum said,
'Or you will be punished and sent off to bed.'

Next day naughty Jimmy, his mum disobeyed,
Into the frog pond, quite deep he did wade.

When he opened his mouth to take a deep breath,
A fat tadpole swam in, nearly choked him to death.

He coughed and he spluttered, the tadpole flew out
Into the mouth of a very big trout.

Trout swam after Jimmy and bit his big toe,
Jim ran home to Mum with a long tale of woe.

His mum said, 'I warned you, it serves you quite right!
You're a very bad boy - get out of my sight!'

To his room Jim was sent by his mum, out of spite,
She told him, 'You'll go without dinner tonight.'

'I won't go to the pond anymore,' Jimmy said,
'Next time I'll go to the river instead.'

Seems he's not learnt his lesson, I think you'll agree,
So what happens next? We must just wait and see.

Iris Melville

The Birds And The Bumblebee

A cheeky little sparrow met a pompous bumblebee,
'Hello,' said the sparrow, 'hello and chirrupee!'
The fat and pompous bumblebee just looked him up and down,
And with his nose up in the air, he flew away to town.

The cheeky little sparrow thought, *he shan't treat me like that!*
And flew off to the marketplace to have a chitter-chat.
He gathered all his friends around and asked them what to do
And when they had arranged a plan, they went off two by two.

A little later on that day they met the bumblebee.
The little sparrows tittered, 'Tee-hee-hee, hee-hee!'
They stalked behind the bumblebee and when they saw their chance,
They pecked him and they teased him and really made him dance.

So now whenever that bumblebee meets the little sparrow,
His manners he remembers and politely greets, 'Good morrow.'
He is no longer pompous, that fat old bumblebee,
But always nods his head and smiles. 'Good day, good day,' says he.

Ann Voaden

Pablo Picasso

Pablo Picasso
Came to tea.
While eating cake
He painted me
In cadmium red
And ultramarine.
It took me all night
To get myself clean.

Joe Hoyle

Christmas Night

Hush my little ones, I can hear
The jingle bells and time is near
For Santa and his reindeer sleigh
Coming from lands so far away.
Tomorrow will come and at dawn's light
Christmas Day will be big and bright
For all the children to enjoy
The birth of Jesus, the baby boy.

Hush my little ones, go to sleep
Under the bedclothes, do not peep
Santa's coming, I am listening
On the rooftops frost is glistening.
The whispers of the girls and boys
Of Santa's sack filled with toys
Tomorrow for Jesus we must pray
On his birthday, Christmas Day.

P Evans

The Penguin

Plip-plop went the penguin
Down the slippery slope.
But could he glide
Back up the slide?
The penguin had to hope.

Slip-slop went the penguin
Gearing up the run.
He held his breath
Just two steps left
And then there was just one.

Flip-flop went the penguin
Making it to the top.
A leap in the air
A missed step there
And down again with a plop.

Natalie Pryor

Soapbox Derby

Jamie woke up early, sunshine in his room,
He was so excited now, it's all going to happen soon,
Jamie enjoyed his breakfast, though he did not make it last.
He grabbed his coat and helmet, then ran outside real fast.
Lifting the plastic cover, revealing the great machine,
It was sleek, just like a Ferrari and polished to a sheen.
Today was the soapbox derby, Jamie was going to win,
He'd oiled the wheels and steering, then painted the wood and tin.
Proudly pushing his chariot out into the lane then up the hill,
Not a breath of wind was blowing, the world was calm and still.
Jamie soon arrived at the start line, dozens of boys were there,
Then five, four, three, two, one, they were off without a care.
The first bend was a tight one, Jamie skidded round in his kart,
Gripping the steering wheel tightly, could feel the pounding of
his heart,
As the machines they gathered momentum, all jostling for position,
Jamie got his wheels in front of them, passing all the opposition.
Then as they approached the finishing line, one of Jamie's
tyres burst,
But Jamie wrestled to control his kart and crossed the finish line first.
All the boys gathered round him, shouting and cheering, all
sweating and damp,
They wanted to shake our Jamie's hand, cos Jamie was the
soapbox champ.

Geoff Donkin

Octopuzzle

It's fun to be an octopus,
Though sometimes there's confusion.
Should I wear four pairs of gloves,
Or put four pairs of shoes on?

Sharon Tregenza

First Haircut

I've been told I'll have to visit the barber,
Have my hair cut 'just like my father'
No way are they going to get me in there -
They have men's heads in the windows that just stare!

I'd scream and cry as much as I could,
Don't care one bit how my hair looks.
I am not going in - I'm full of dread,
I know I'll come out without my head.

I'm only little - but it's not hard to know,
It's a funny old world in which to grow.
Grown-ups are very, very confusing,
They look at me and think *I'm* amusing!

Davina Headland

Marvin The Monster And The Lost Sky-Blue Cap

When Marvin the monster lay down for his nap,
He was wearing his favourite old sky-blue cap.
But when he awoke it was gone from his head
And he found an old, red, woolly hat there instead.

He went to his mother and tugged on her skirt:
'Did you take my hat?' (He sounded quite hurt.)
'Your old sky-blue cap? Of course not!' she said.
'I last saw that old thing on top of your head!'

Next Marvin went to his sister, Martine,
Lying on her bed reading a magazine.
'Have you seen my old sky-blue cap?' he asked her.
'It's gone from my head and it's just a disaster.'

She flicked her green fringe and glared down at him,
'Why would I want it? You really are dim.'
She went back to reading with a snort of disdain,
So Marvin turned around and left again.

He found his dad sawing wood in the shed,
With a cap just like Marvin's old one on his head.
Marvin yelled over the sound of the saw,
'Is that my hat? I'm sure that I've seen it before.'

'No, this blue cap is mine,' Marvin's dad said.
'It'll be far too big for your little head.'
But Marvin tried it on anyway (just to check)
And found that it covered his head to the neck.

Marvin went to his room, he was very upset,
He'd looked everywhere and not found it yet.
Leaning over the bed frame, he hung his green head,
When what should be spy down the side of his bed?

A glimpse of sky-blue? Yes, it was his cap.
It must have fallen off during his nap!
He fitted it on with the peak at the rear,
His best sky-blue cap with the holes for his ears.

Alice Thomas

Wet Weather

As I peered through my bedroom windowpane
Upon the sodden garden down below
I wondered, will the roses bloom again?

I'm weary of this everlasting, saturating rain
That depresses my youthful spirit so
As I peer through my bedroom windowpane.

When swirling waters vainly seek a drain
In which to disappear, down which to go,
I wonder, will the roses bloom again?

And yet the sun will surely shine again!
Despite what I see, in my heart I know
As I peer through my bedroom windowpane.

But until then, with agony and pain,
Which blow away my spirit leaving sadness and woe,
I wonder, will the roses bloom again?

But if extremely patient I remain
Life will itself tell of its ebbs and flows
As I peer through my bedroom windowpane
And wonder, will the roses bloom again?

Dan Pugh

Where The Angels Hide

Where the angels hide
Where they choose to play
In the sky above
On the most beautiful day
With their wings open wide
With gold-dusted feathers they glide.

In a bed of soft red roses they smile
In a field of daisies they hide and seek
Where the waterfalls in a hidden paradise they greet.

Over the moon and with a shooting star they dance
With wings open far they sway and prance
In the midnight hour flying high and low
With invisible wings some might not know.

Where the rainbow ends they lay
With a chest of ancient treasure some might say
Wearing a golden-dusted coat
In a cotton wool cloud they float.

When the sun beams down like a golden glow
Onto those gold-feathered wings
Which sparkle like a diamond in the sky
That's when you'll know.

Camille Miriam Metcalfe

Tick, Tick, Tick

Tick, tick, tick
The clock is ticking
It works with gears and cogs
As cogs crush against one another, it ticks
As it ticks, seconds go by
As it ticks, it says something
Child, you ought to know
Listen to the tick of the clock
And think about how much we love you.

Ayo Oyeku

My Friend The Frog

O little dog, don't chase the frog,
He's done no harm to you.
He hops along and croaks his song,
So let him live here too.

Among the fish he'll splash and splish,
They all get on so well.
The pond's his home, no need to roam,
He'll stay here for a spell.

His friends call round, to leap and bound,
Amid the dewy grass.
Play hide-and-seek three times a week,
How quickly days do pass.

He'll find a wife, sometime in life,
And she will live here too.
She'll lay some eggs and they'll grow legs,
As tadpoles always do.

So little dog, be kind to frog,
Because he is my friend.
We'll all have fun beneath the sun,
Till playtime has to end.

Wendy Wilson

Randal's Scandal

There was a young fellow called Randal
Whose habit caused quite a large scandal
For he picked at his ears
Until after three years
He had enough wax for a candle.

Alec Sillifant

Magic

Christmas baubles on Christmas trees
Stars and reindeer, of those there are quite a few.
Different colours for everyone to see
Round shapes, lantern shapes, large, fat shapes too.

There are snowflake shapes and boot shapes
Red bows and gold tinsel as well.
Miniature parcels and silver angels
Holly leaves with some berries and some little bells.

A moving Santa sits in a shop window
His sleigh all shiny and red.
His red sack overflowing the presents
His reindeer by his helpers are led.

Elves with pointed hats on
In green colours and also red.
Snowmen with scarves and hats on
Children gasp at the sights they have shared.

Christmas turkey, Christmas pudding, mince pies
Sherry trifle, double cream and brandy sauce.
Christmas hats, Christmas crackers, Christmas carols
And Christmas cards of course.

Christmas presents we exchange with pleasure
Our families as happy as can be.
Children race to see their surprises
Christmas Day is for all of us you see.

Some people say it's too commercial
Just done to make us spend and spend.
But if you take the magic out of Christmas
It would be like losing a friend.

H Dormand

The Flea And The Dog

The dog was feeling lonely
When a flea jumped on its back
It said, 'I've come to join you
As it's company that you lack
You want to get out more
The fresh air will do you good'
'I would like to,' said the little dog
'But I'm stuffed and made of wood'
The flea said, 'I'll have to leave you
As I need fresh air too
If I jump on a bus I may find
One going to the zoo
And when I get there
Perhaps I will see
That one of the animals
Will welcome my company.'

Diana Daley

The Curse

One day when we were running, running
On our way to school
We saw a little woman
On a three-legged stool
At the side of the pavement
While the people all walked past
An old witch woman
From somewhere in the past.
She was sitting with her knitting
On a three-legged stool
While we were running
Running to school.

Robert said hello to her and I did too
But naughty little Cicily said, 'Silly old moo!
You're an ugly old woman, as ugly as can be
Such an ugly old woman as there never ought to be.'

The little old woman waved a needle in the air
And at that very moment Cicily was not there!
She wasn't on the ground, she wasn't in the air
We looked, looked, looked and looked - she wasn't anywhere!

We've all looked really hard for her
Every single day
But there isn't any sign of her -
She's vanished clean away.
We'd ask the knitting woman
If she would undo the curse
But we're scared we might annoy her
And she might do something worse!

Fred Brown

Sweet Innocence

The little boy ran down the road, his hoop was just ahead -
And with a stick was hitting it, as more and more it sped.
Until quite naturally he stopped, fain gasping there for air,
But sad to say, the hoop raced on down to the village square.
Upon the green a bring-and-buy had just by chance begun,
With trestle tables, chock-a-block and people having fun.
There's homemade jams and marmalades and wines and cakes
and tea,
A beer tent for the gentlemen, a sort of jamboree.
The rector of the parish said on opening the 'do',
How gratifying it was to see so many people who -
He's sure would empt' their pockets out for such a worthwhile cause,
Then praised the Women's Institute afore a fleeting pause -
Suddenly, an almighty crash and mayhem mowed them flat,
The tables had all doubled up and on the grass were splat.
The tent and beer, and barbecue and jams and wines and cakes -
Were interspersed with tea and buns and strawberry milkshakes.
The public and the parson too, were knotted in a group -
Whenas a small voice, anxious, asked, 'Please, have you seen
my hoop?'

Derek Haskett-Jones

Baby Black, The Bold Bunny

This is the tale of a rabbit who lives near Ashcourt Drive
And was born the runt of the litter, so is lucky to be alive.
He's known by the name of Baby Black, whose idea I cannot tell,
Maybe it came from Lauren, or perhaps it was Annabel.
Poor bunny lost his parents at a very early age,
It soon became clear, without them, he would not live in their cage.
No! A house rabbit he decided, that's what he wanted to be,
To visit all the bedrooms or sit on someone's knee.
A very determined rabbit, who'll get just what he needs,
Helping himself to nibbles, in-between his proper feeds.
At night he might sleep with Lauren in her comfy little bed,
Then he'd nip over and visit Annabel, try her bed out instead!
He'd have to avoid 'Big Philip' who might just put him in a pie
But he could rely on Lesley, to give him an alibi.
Still, life he finds enjoyable, a bunny of simple tastes,
Like apples, crisps and nuts, in fact, nothing goes to waste.
The television with its trailing wires that look a tasty treat,
How about those furry slippers? Yes! he could eat both feet!
Their house is very friendly, lots of creatures, lots of talk,
But when will they buy a lead and collar and take him out for a walk?
When the cleaner comes to visit, it's wise not to get under her feet,
It's safe in the conservatory where he lies beneath a seat.
He's a creature of distinction and he's a creature of habit,
So don't be offensive by saying . . . he's really just a rabbit!

Lindsey Priest

My Little Brother

My brother's name is Leslie, he bugs me all day long,
He wants my toys, games and stuff
And tells on me to Mum.

He draws faces on my posters, puts spiders in my socks,
Plays frisbees with my CDs,
Help, I need a lock!

He finds my diary I've hidden and shows it to my dad,
He makes me oh so cross,
I feel I am going mad.

But when I'm feeling lonely and sometimes a bit sad,
My little brother hugs me
And then things don't feel that bad.

Vannessa Boom

Toys

My Bombley-Wombley and my Fubbley-Wubbley
Are my favourite playtime pair.
The Fubbley-Wubbley is all covered in fur
And the Bombley-Wombley has a head with no hair.
Fubbley-Wubbley goes to bed with me
And lives in my little cot,
And Bombley shares my bath with me
And bounces and splashes a lot.
Bombley is a rubber toy
With a big, round head and limbs like wobbly pegs,
And Fubbley has a safety pin to hold his fur, but has no legs.
Bombley's eyes are painted blue,
But Fubbley's green glass ones stare at you.
Bombley was found on a car boot stall,
But Mummy made Fubbley with glass eyes and all.
Bombley-Wombley and Fubbley-Wubbley
Both go with me everywhere.
They are my very favourite things -
Except for my teddy bear!

Betty Margaret Irwin-Burton

A Gift Of Love

Children are like flowers that in your garden grow
They are made from love and loving as everyone will know.
They bring such joy and gladness within the hearts of men
And as we watch them growing, we pause a while and then
The years they are so fleeting, they are not children long
They soon grow into manhood and join in life's glad song.
So relish ye your children, the gift of God above
They bring such joy to all mankind and fill our hearts with love.

June Clare

The Enormous Chocolate House

Along the winding block-paved path, around the first winding bend
Thomas and Megan met their first important friend.

Minty, a rusty-brown, long-haired dog
With huge, bright, sparkling eyes
He could sniff his way to chocolate - they soon did realise.

Along the winding block-paved path, around the second
winding bend
Thomas and Megan met another important friend.

A huge, long-legged, hairy spider
With the biggest smile they had ever seen
But he was a friendly spider, he was not mean.

Along the winding block-paved path, around the very last
winding bend
There was an enormous chocolate house, built right at the end.

Everything was made of chocolate
It was so hard to believe
Even the garden gates and all the trees and leaves.

They ate and ate until they could not eat any more
Then they saw the very tall giant standing at the door.

He was very cross that they should eat without his permission
So he gave each and every one of them a punishing mission
They had to collect all the chocolate leaves and place them in
a barrel
And if they should disobey him, it would be at their peril.

But in the skies above, came another important friend
It was Beagle the Eagle on whom they could depend
On being safely rescued, on his wings he flew them home
Perhaps they will now think twice before they decide to roam.

Along the winding block-paved path, around the very last
winding bend
There was an enormous chocolate house built right at the end
Everything was made of chocolate
It was so hard to believe
Even the garden gate and all the trees and leaves.

Everything was made of chocolate
It was so hard to believe
Even the garden gate and all the trees and leaves.

Everything was made of chocolate
It was so hard to believe
Even the garden gate and all the trees and leaves.

Rita Bridgman

Saving Graces

When Great Uncle Charles had finished his cuppa
He lectured his nieces, those he bullied at supper
What keeps me so young and immature in my life
Is poetry first then my trouble and strife

Just dip into Shelley, Shakespeare or Donne
And find how your mind and thoughts come undone
Imagine their time and the state of the Earth
The mystery and misery try the life of a serf

What pleasure they had you could count on one hand
No painkillers, hospitals or docs in the land
Just a lot of religion to keep you on track
So when your time came he wouldn't send you straight back

Plunge deep in the pool of verse, prose and rhyme
Escape to this world of an earlier time
And while splashing around in the shallow end first
That's where you'll find Uncle Charles and his verse

Start your journey from here you trio of graces
Feel the warmth and the pain from those earlier races
Whatever your thoughts write them down in prose
Join hands with my soulmates, let's find where it goes.

Charles Keeble

Pixies, Elves And Gnomes

If you're in the garden
And you should chance to see
A funny little pixie
Just watch him quietly.
His coat and cap is yellow
His shoes of brightest green
And his beard, you're sure to notice
Is the longest beard you've seen.
He's loved by all the fairies
And friends with all the gnomes
And all the folk in fairyland
Invite him to their homes.
We don't know what his name is
For no one ever tells
The names of little fairy folk
Who live in flower bells.

Doris Mary Miller

Would Mum Teach Me Like This?

All time run around
And never keep still
When you don't want to go to school
Pretend you are ill

Eat all the sweets
And leave vegetables behind
Say spiteful words to people
And never be kind

Play tricks on your teachers
And pretend it wasn't you
Be very naughty at school
And bossy too

Turn on the television
And watch it all day
Don't do your homework
Instead go out and play

It's too early for bed
Stay awake and play with your Game Boy
Don't brush your teeth
Just think your toothbrush is a toy

Don't share things with friends
Always be mean
When someone needs help
You act like nothing was seen

Wherever you are
Push people around
Don't worry about rubbish
Just throw it on the ground

What do you think?
Would Mum teach me like this?
Or all these lessons
She will dismiss.

Marinela Reka

Cardboard Tube

A cardboard tube
played your voice in all its vowels
across your palate;
hidden within its base.

Then playing the trumpet
held above the L-shape of your arm,
or maybe a speaker;
disconnected from its mic.

It laughs in your voice,
momentarily disengaged
for you to catch breath,
before looking down its long shank;

snippets viewed in single-shot mode
captured in memories frame.

Your oval view;
part picture, part jigsaw;
knowing our lives are complete
however fragmented the world may look.

Simon Jones

Summer Gone

This summer gone my family spent a fortnight by the sea
Mum and Dad, Auntie Lou, the triplets, Gran and me
Dad found a special offer on a six-berth caravan
And we all squashed in together, like sardines in a can

Mum did what she always does; cooked and cleaned and shopped
Dad helped with the triplets and their whining never stopped
Auntie put a deckchair on a patch of grass outside
And whiled away the hours until the blazing sun had died

No sooner we'd unpacked our stuff than me and Gran were gone
We climbed aboard an open bus that went along the prom
First stop was the fairground and she's on before I know
Her favourite was the dodgems - you should have seen her go!

She bought us each a candyfloss, two giant clouds of fluff
We climbed the helter-skelter - boy, was I out of puff!
But Gran was so excited and sped down without a care
And when she reached the bottom she had candyfloss for hair

We queued for quite a while for fish and chips with mushy peas
Mum was very cross cos she'd already made our teas
She sent us off to bed as we were getting in the way
But Gran and me were happy as we'd had a smashing day

I climbed into the bottom bunk as Gran baggsed the top
She had a stash of goodies; sweets and crisps and pop
On the stroke of midnight, outside we quietly crept
And beneath the stars we feasted while everybody slept

The next day came a message that my grandpa wasn't well
Gran would have to leave us; she was worried I could tell
She insisted we should stay because we'd only just begun
But I knew that Gran's departure meant the end of all the fun . . .

This summer gone my family spent a fortnight by the sea
But the best day was the first when it was just my gran and me.

Pauline Williams

The Treat

Trick or treat night just beginning.
Goblins in the wood are grinning.
They lurk or leer among the trees
Or down they squat, hugging their knees
While in the red-gold sky, clouds roll
Over a bridge where troll meets troll.

The twins lose some of their poise.
In the undergrowth a scuffling noise.
Far off, then nearer, a growling
From a red-eyed, black beast prowling
Ready to sink fangs into prey
And drag it bloodily away.

The trolls give each other a nudge,
'For twins - or for beast - *we* won't budge
Tonight from no one we're hidden
Crossing our bridge is forbidden.'
When one twin makes a sudden dash
The other hears such a loud *splash!*

Troll thrown where the stream is flowing
That boy fears the beast - eyes glowing.
With slavering jaws - not a friend.
Gleeful goblins await his end.
The twin with dry feet starts to yell,
'Trolls! It's your fault my brother fell.

If you'll save him from the Hell Hound
Come with us when we're homeward-bound.
We'll give you the food in our fridge
O troll - guardian of the bridge!'

'Good thinking, we'll accept your food.'
Trolls flung the beast back in the wood.

Chris Creedon

Moving On

From little school to big school,
Enjoying the big time,
Small time's no longer mine.

Everyone is back at school,
New subjects, new rules,
Evening time's no longer mine.

Alex Forsyth (12)

My Garden

My garden is a quiet place with lawns and many trees,
Flower beds and borders fair and seats to rest at ease.
Sit quiet and in the border glance, you very well may see,
Fairies, elves and pixies bright, all dancing round with glee.
The elves and pixies make their suits from leaves, all shades of green,
While fairies have the prettiest gowns of colours quite serene.
There's marigold and roses fair, some lovely lilies too,
And skirts all made from bluebells in lovely shades of blue.
These little folk are very shy and often hide away,
But you'll make them very happy if you wish them all good-day.

D J Wooding

Emma's Prayer

(Dedicated to Emma Jayne Garlick)

Dear Jesus, thank you for a lovely day
Please bless and love my mummy and daddy,
Did you see the fun I had with Nanny when she came?
Mummy said you would in your own way,
When I get my goodnight kiss from my nanny,
She says to me, 'God bless you, my little lamb,'
Jesus, when I lay me down to sleep,
Can I see the angel who tends your sheep?
Amen.

John Clarke

Forward Press Information

We hope you have enjoyed reading this book - and that you will continue to enjoy it in the coming years.

If you like reading and writing poetry drop us a line, or give us a call, and we'll send you a free information pack.

Alternatively if you would like to order further copies of this book or any of our other titles, then please give us a call or log onto our website at www.forwardpress.co.uk

Forward Press Ltd. Information
Remus House
Coltsfoot Drive
Peterborough
PE2 9JX

(01733) 898101